BITCOIN
THE POW
HOLDS

All You Need to Know About Harnessing the Power of Bitcoin

Jerry Ryder

Dear Treasured Reader,

Thank you so much for purchasing a copy of "Bitcoin and the Power It Holds". I hope you get exactly what you were looking for in this book and so much more.

If you would be so kind as to leave a review on the platform that you purchased this book from if you liked/enjoyed it at any point in your reading, I would really appreciate that.

If you have any topics and suggestions that you would like included in the book to help solve any problems/queries that were not addressed with regards to Bitcoin, do feedback in the review as well.

Thank You Once Again!

TABLE OF CONTENTS

INTRODUCTION

Bitcoin is taking over the world. This digital currency is completely different than anything that we have seen in the past, which makes it new and exciting. There are also a lot of cool benefits that come with this currency, such as the ability to be able to send money all over the world with low transactions fees, keeping your personal information safe and secure, and not having to deal with government intervention.

Despite the growing popularity that comes with Bitcoin, there are still a lot of people who do not understand what this digital currency is all about. They may have heard about it in the past, but if they were asked to explain it to someone else, they might be confused on where to start. This guidebook is going to spend some time talking about Bitcoin and helping you to better understand what goes on with this digital currency.

Inside this guidebook, we are going to talk about a lot of the different aspects that come with Bitcoin and using this network. We will talk about some of the basics of Bitcoin such as what it is, the benefits of using it, how to decide if the risks are worth the benefits, how to get your own Bitcoin, and even how to make money on this network. We will also spend some time talking about the blockchain technology that helps this whole program run smoothly and efficiently.

Digital currencies have started to take over the world. They are responsible for allowing people to exchange products and money no matter where they are located. Even though they are relatively new, they are something that will keep on growing and changing the way that we do business, especially when it comes to working with the blockchain network that runs most digital currencies.

When you are ready to learn a bit more about Bitcoin and how to interact with this network, make sure to check out this guidebook so you can start to understand all of the parts that go with it.

PART ONE:

WHAT YOU NEED TO

KNOW ABOUT BITCOIN

CHAPTER 1: WHAT IS BITCOIN

To get started, the first thing that we need to concentrate on is what is Bitcoin? It is important to understand what this is all about before we can move on to the other parts for how to use Bitcoin. Bitcoin is a digital currency that is created and used completely online. You will not be able to print Bitcoin and carry it around, and there is no central agency that is in charge of controlling it. People will be able to produce the Bitcoins, as can companies with the help of a software that can solve mathematical problems.

Bitcoin may not have been the very first attempt at a decentralized currency, but it is the first major one that became successful. What makes it different from traditional currencies though? Bitcoin is similar to traditional currencies in that you can use the coins you have to make online purchases, which is something that traditional currencies have been doing for some time.

However, there are some big differences with this digital currency. The biggest way that it is different from traditional currency is that it is considered decentralized. There isn't one institution that will control the network, which is something that a lot of people enjoy because it means that the government and big banks are not able to control their money and the way that they decide to spend that money.

Many people wonder who created Bitcoin in the first place. Satoshi Nakamoto was the developer who proposed Bitcoin, but no one knows who this person is or what group of people were in charge o it. The idea of Bitcoin was to come up with a form of payment online that could be based on a mathematical proof, rather than on a bank or government entity. The idea here was to make a new currency that was free from any central authority (which is completely different from some of the traditional currencies that we have come to use). This currency was also supposed to be transferable electronically without all of the waits and would provide an alternative that could provide low transaction fees.

One thing to remember is that no one is in charge of printing out the Bitcoin currency. In fact, this currency is not on that can be physically printed at all. You can only use this currency to make purchases and send money online, but you will never be able to print out the currency to use in that way.

Instead, you can join in on the Bitcoin network to get your own Bitcoin. This is a community that anyone can use right now. The new Bitcoin are added to the network when something is mined, which is done using the computing power of a distributed network. This network also helps to process transactions using the Bitcoins, which means that Bitcoin has become its very own payment network.

In addition, you have to realize that it is impossible to churn out an unlimited amount of Bitcoins. Unlike traditional currency where the government or a big bank can decide to print off more currencies whenever they would like, there is a finite amount of Bitcoin available, and no more can ever be produced.

According to the protocol that helps to make Bitcoin run says that it is only possible for 21 million Bitcoins to be created by the miners. The good news is that these coins are easily divided up into smaller parts. The smallest part is one hundred millionth of a Bitcoin, and it is called a Satoshi.

At this point, you may be curious as to what the Bitcoin is based off. When we are talking about traditional currencies, we know that they are going to be based on gold or silver. In theory, if you took a dollar to the bank, you would be able to get a bit of gold back based on the value of the dollar at the time. While you would not actually be able to do this, it is the basis of traditional currencies. However, Bitcoin is not a currency that is based on gold and silver, but it is based on mathematics.

When Bitcoin was released, not all of the coins were released. This means that not all of the 21 million coins are available in the world right now. The miners will need to get to work to release some more of coins when they are ready. They can do this by using a software program that will work on a specified mathematical formula to produce these Bitcoins.

It is possible to go through and find this mathematical formula easily because it is freely available and anyone can check it out. It is also an open sourced software, which means that anyone can take a look at it and ensure that it is going to behave in the manner that it should. Of course, there are a few other rules that come into place when mining the coins. Otherwise, all the coins would be mined out quickly as each person would jump on this quickly.

So, now you may be curious as to what are some of the characteristics of Bitcoin, what makes it stand out from the crowd and makes it such a great currency to work with. Some of the characteristics that come with Bitcoin include:

- It is decentralized: this network does not have one authority that will control it. Each computer that joins the network will be able to become a miner if they would like to, but there isn't anyone who can come into the market and decide the value of the coins or take the coins away.

- Easy to set up: when working with traditional banks, you can find that getting set up can be hard. You may have to jump through some hops just to open up your bank account, and if you want to work on a merchant account, it could be hard as well. With Bitcoin, you can sign up in just a few seconds, without a lot of questions, and you will not have to pay any fees.

- Anonymous: many users like to go with this option because it can keep their information safe when they are online. Their Bitcoin addresses will not be linked to their names, addresses or any other personal information. you do need to take some extra steps to make sure that your information is completely safe, but it is much better than the current methods that traditional banks use.

- Transparent: even though you can keep your information safe on the Bitcoin network, Bitcoin is also going to store details of all transactions that occur on this network on the blockchain. Anyone who has joined the network can take a look at blockchain to see what has been going on.

- Low fees: when you make payments, send money to people in other countries, and so on, they are going to charge you some high fees to get things done. This is not something that you have to deal with on Bitcoin. If you need to do a lot of transactions internationally, this may be the network that you want to work with.

- Fast: with traditional banking, it can take days for information to go from your account over to the other account. With Bitcoin, you can send money anywhere in the world, and it will show up there just a few minutes later.

- Non-repudiable: once you send out some money on the Bitcoin network, the transaction is done. You will not be able to get this money back unless the recipient agrees to send the money back to you.

Signing up for the Bitcoin network is pretty easy. You simply need to sign up for a Bitcoin address and have a wallet to hold onto your coins. There are several great options that are available for doing this, and you can pick out the option that is the best for your needs. You will then use your address anytime that someone is supposed to send you money or any time that you are supposed to make a purchase or send money.

You will also need to make some exchanges to turn your traditional money over to Bitcoin so you can begin exchanging. You can do mining or just start to sell your own products online, but most people decide to work with some kind of exchange, such as what is found with Coinbase and some other options, to keep things easy. Once you exchange out your traditional currencies and turn them into Bitcoin, you can start doing any transaction that you would like.

Working with Bitcoin is a great way to make purchases online, save money, and see some that trade and commerce do not have to be quite as difficult as some of the big banks and governments make it feel with traditional methods. Bitcoin is providing the solutions that a lot of people are looking for.

CHAPTER 2: A HISTORY OF BITCOIN

We just spent some time talking about what Bitcoin is and why it is gaining so much in popularity recently. But what we haven't spent time talking about is some of the histories of Bitcoin. Where did this kind of coin come from? Who came up with the idea of the Bitcoin and do we really know why they decided to go with an online form of currency? Let's stop and take some time to look at the interesting, although short, of the Bitcoin currency.

Bitcoin was created by a group or an individual; it is still uncertain, that likes to use the pseudonym of Satoshi Nakamoto. In November of 2008, Nakamoto wrote and published a paper on a website that described Bitcoin and how this online currency would work. This individual claimed to be someone from Japan, but upon further research, it was shown that no one really even knew who this person, or group of people, was.

The idea of Bitcoin became public during 2008, but the idea of an online currency that wasn't controlled by the government had been around since the Internet began. There were many programmers and leaders who had tried to make one of these currencies. One example of this, Ecash, was launched earlier on and it tried to gain success, but it failed.

The idea behind Bitcoin was different than the others. While the others still tried to use government agencies and traditional forms of banks, Bitcoin was going to get rid of government interference and would instead rely on a community and peer-to-peer currency to work. They would set up a ledger, which is known as the blockchain, that could track all the Bitcoin that was created and would record the transactions while making sure that the users would be protected.

It didn't take long for the ideas that were presented started to gain some followers, although, in the beginning, most of these were computer experts. In 2009, the first 50 Bitcoins were created. It was through the process of Bitcoin mining that companies and users would be able to create more Bitcoin by solving hard equations with their computers to help keep the network safe.

To be truthful, the idea of Bitcoin came at the perfect time, which is going to contribute to how successful the currency was. In 2008 and 2009, Bitcoin was brand new, but the financial markets all around the world were suffering and about to collapse. As this crisis continued to go on, many economic leaders and even central banks were being overwhelmed and couldn't keep up with the developments that they were seeing. The confidence levels of the consumer in traditional currencies went down, and people were already questioning the value of these national currencies.

This made it a natural draw when Bitcoin was first released. People were tired of the mess that the government was making and they like the idea of an online currency that the government couldn't control and that would not be influenced by how the economy was doing at the time.

During the first few years, Nakamoto added in some guidance and insights to the earliest of Bitcoin miners to help them learn how to make the system work. But by December of 2010, he published his final message and then hasn't been heard of since then. Despite Nakamoto disappearing, Bitcoin has continued to grow over the years.

By the end of January 2011, there was estimated to have been more than 5 million Bitcoins that were mined, and this currency was beginning to see attention all across the globe. Bitcoin exchanges were growing, which allowed users to trade their national currencies for Bitcoin and the other way around. Bitcoin was growing fast, and people were paying attention.

Then in 2013, there was a period of instability that came with Bitcoins. During this time, the value of Bitcoin surged to record highs before it crashed down in just a few days. Many believe that this is a sign that Bitcoin is still having some troubles and that it could end up failing if this does not end up getting fixed. But so far, Bitcoin has been running successfully, and we have yet to see if it will stand the test of time.

Since that time, Bitcoin has continued to grow, and more people all throughout the world can join this exchange. If you have a computer and some money to exchange, you can join the Bitcoin network. This is part of the reason that international trading is so popular on this network. It allows people to meet and sell products no matter where they are located, and they will not have to deal with the high transaction fees that come with traditional financial institutions along the way.

There are many reasons that people are falling in love with the Bitcoin network. Some chose to join because they were still worried about the volatile economy that was going on when Bitcoin started – which still hasn't gone away completely.

Still, others have their own reasons. They may like to have a currency that does not have the government all around making demands and changing the worth of the currency. Some like to be able to shop online without their personal information being readily available online like it would be with other forms of shopping. Some like the idea of making purchases or sending money overseas without having to worry about all of those high fees or what the exchange rate is at the time.

And of course, there are some people who have chosen to get into Bitcoin because it is a good investment opportunity for them. With the high value of Bitcoin as this time, it makes sense that some people are trying to see if they can make some money in the process.

Since the beginning of Bitcoin, things have changed quite a bit. This was just a general idea, one that had been tried out in the past and was a failure. But Bitcoin changed the way that things were done, and it did make an impact. Thanks to the blockchain technology that was behind it, and the help of the right timing, Bitcoin has spread all around the globe and is becoming more popular each day.

CHAPTER 3:

WHAT IS BLOCKCHAIN AND HOW DOES IT HELP BITCOIN RUN?

While there are a few different types of software that help to run the Bitcoin network, one of the most important has to the blockchain. This is the ledger that is going to hold onto all transactions that occur inside of this network and will also keep the information safe and secure from hackers and outside sources. Without this technology being in place, it would be impossible for anyone to trust the Bitcoin network, and it would never have gotten as popular as it is.

The blockchain is basically a type of database that is responsible for holding onto anything of value. In terms of how it works on the Bitcoin network, this database is going to hold onto all of the transactions that occur on Bitcoin, including payments received money sent, and purchases. This helps the users to be able to complete transactions on the system without having to rely on a third party at all.

Blockchain and Bitcoin are two completely different types of technologies, but without blockchain, it would be so hard for people to trust the Bitcoin network at all. It was hard to convince people in the first place that they should send money online and not have a bank or a financial company behind the money. Yes, when the economy was failing, it was easier to get people to check out Bitcoin and this online currency, but without blockchain, it would have had a much harder time getting started

The blockchain can help out in a variety of ways. First, it can hold onto anything of value. With the Bitcoin network, it is going to hold onto currency, but it can also be used to hold onto smart contracts, titles, and so much more. With all of these applications, it is no wonder that so much attention is being given to blockchain platforms and technology right now

Working with the blockchain technology is pretty simple, even though the underlying workings of it may be more complicated. For someone who is just using the Bitcoin network, blockchain is simply a ledger they can look at to check on their transactions and make sure that everything is in order. But the fact that we can do all of this without a bank or another institution is pretty amazing.

So, let's take a look at how blockchain is going to work inside of the Bitcoin network. To start, you will need to sign up for the Bitcoin network. This is pretty easy to work on, just make sure that you pick out a unique and secure address so that others are not able to easily identify you with all of your transactions.

As soon as you sign up for the Bitcoin network, you are going to receive a new block from the blockchain. This block is for you to use and it will automatically fill up with all of the transactions that you do while you are on the Bitcoin network. This can include any kind of transaction that you can think of, including currency, titles, insurance information, contracts, and so on.

Each person will get to fill up the block depending on how many transactions they complete at a time. Some people will spend a lot of time on the network and can get a lot of transactions done quickly. Others may choose to just use this system on occasion, and their transactions will not be as many. The block is set up to hold a set number of transactions so how quickly it fills up with depending on how much you use it.

Once the block has filled up, it is going to join in with the permanent record so that it can stay safe. Once it joins this permanent record, it becomes impossible for changes to be made, which helps to keep your security on the network. You will then receive a new block to start working on.

After you have a few of blocks, they are going to form their own blockchain. You can go back to look through the blockchain any time that you would like. So, if you would like to look and see what transactions you have done in the past, it would be easy to accomplish with the blockchain. Each person will have their own personal blockchain that contains all of the transactions that they have ever done on the Bitcoin network.

In addition, their personal blockchain will be added into the main blockchain that comes with the Bitcoin network. This chain will have all the blocks from all the users on the network, keeping them all in order and safe. As these individual blockchains start to add the main network's chain, miners will come in to add unique hashes to each chain, keeping the information safe and making it easy to see if someone tried to mess with any of the information.

Understanding how the blockchain works can be a bit of a challenge. To keep things simple, we can think of it in terms of something that we are familiar with, such as our bank statements. Each block that you receive will be like your monthly bank statement (although these blocks will hold a certain amount of transactions rather than focusing on a certain amount of time). This block will keep filling up with all of the transactions that you do over time, and you can go back through and look at your information anytime that you need to review something.

After you have a few of these blocks or monthly statements, they are going to link together to make your records. You can still go through and read the information that you want, but as each statement or block gets added into the permanent record, it cannot be changed at all, helping it to stay secure.

There are quite a few applications of this kind of blockchain technology, and it is going to continue to grow into the future. Right now, in addition to working with Bitcoin and other digital currencies, there are already platforms that are being developed to use blockchain with insurance, banks, the financial industry, and even with digital voting.

Blockchain is quickly changing the way that our world is going to work in the future. It is fast, getting payments done in a few minutes rather than in a few days like it does in the regular financial institution. In addition, it is secure, will show the transparency that you need, and so much more. But when it comes to helping out the Bitcoin network, it is one of the most important software available.

PART 2:

SHOULD YOU

INVEST IN

BITCOIN?

CHAPTER 4: BENEFITS OF BITCOIN

There are quite a few benefits that are found when you choose to work with the Bitcoin network. This would seem to make sense as most people would not choose to go on a network that was not able to benefit them in some way. You could choose this network because it is a good investment strategy or you may just like the idea of shopping online without everyone, whether it is a hacker or the government, being able to see what you are doing. This chapter is going to take some time to discuss the various benefits that come with joining the Bitcoin network.

Easy to use

The Bitcoin network is really easy for you to use. You simply need to find an exchange site to work with, so you can transfer your traditional currency over to Bitcoin, and then you are set to go. You can send money, earn money, and make purchases all through this great network. Unlike some other currencies that are hard to exchange and work with, Bitcoin is the complete opposite, allowing you the option to use it without having to worry about the fees and other issues that come with it.

A good investment option

Some people decide to go on the Bitcoin network because it is a great way to invest their money. They can put their money in the Bitcoin company, in the buy and hold strategy, in day trading, and so much more.

It is important to remember though that since Bitcoin is so new, you have to be careful with your investments. It may sound like a good idea because of how much the value in Bitcoin has been rising lately, but Bitcoin really does not have the history to let you know how it would react to various market conditions and when other factors come into play. This is a great investment tool, just make sure you know what you are getting yourself into first.

Low transaction fees

If you wanted to send money to another country to a family member or you want to make a purchase from a store that is not located in your country, you would most likely have to pay a lot of fees. These fees come from the intermediaries that you would have to work with to complete the transaction. They are going to ask for some fees just for doing their job. Plus, the exchange rate can change from day to day, so it is hard to know exactly how much you need to pay.

These transactions can end up costing you a lot of money over time, and most people would much rather learn how to avoid them. With the Bitcoin network, you can send money or make purchases anywhere in the world without having to wait and with the benefit of not having high transaction fees. Not only is the Bitcoin network easy to use, but it can also save you a lot of money as well.

It is faster than other options

When you complete a transaction at your traditional bank or financial institution, how long does it take to complete that transaction? It is likely that those transactions are going to take at least a couple of days to complete through, which can be a pain. You have to wait for the transaction to leave your bank account and then you also have to wait for the seller to receive the funds, which can take a few more days.

The ledgers at most banks and financial institutions are really slow. Each bank is going to deal with its own ledger, so they both have to worry about reconciling it at the end of the day. This can make things really slow, especially if there is a holiday or a weekend that falls in there somewhere.

The blockchain ledger, which helps to run the Bitcoin network, is going to work a bit differently. You will be able to see transactions done almost instantly because you are not relying on two different ledgers, just one main ledger. All transactions on the Bitcoin network can occur through that same ledger, saving a lot of time and hassle in the process.

Blockchain keeps it secure

The blockchain technology is known for keeping all of the Bitcoin networks as secure as possible. It is set up to handle all of the transactions that are allowed on this network and will make it easy to see what transactions you have completed while keeping the information secure.

Blockchain is really a unique kind of ledger. It will get the transactions done in just a few minutes, rather than taking days to complete as we would find with more normal banks and other financial institutions.

There is also the benefit of it being pretty secure. Once transactions are entered into the record on the blockchain, you will not be able to change them. This helps to keep the network secure because no one can go through it later on and make changes or try to commit fraud. It is a much safer system compared to the regular bank ledgers that we are used to dealing with today.

No government interaction

This one is debatable about whether it is a benefit of the Bitcoin network or not and we will discuss both sides in this guidebook. As a benefit, some people enjoy the idea that they can do some of their shopping online without having to worry about the government getting involved.

There are many reasons that people would want to avoid any government interaction in the transactions that they are doing. The first reason is that they may be doing some illegal things online. There are some people who have been able to use the Bitcoin network successfully as a way to purchase and sell items that are illegal, which has given Bitcoin a bit of a bad name in the past. Luckily, most people get on this network to do legitimate trading, so this is not a big issue.

In some countries, the government has started to gain more control over the money, determining how much it is worth from day to day and making it hard to complete some trade. With the help of the Bitcoin network, it is possible to do your own transactions without having to worry about the government influence on the money that you are spending.

As you can see, there are a lot of reasons that people would choose to go with the Bitcoin network. It is safe and effective to use, can help them to keep their information hidden online, and it has the ability to get transactions done quickly. There may be some negatives, but most people really enjoy being able to use a digital currency.

CHAPTER 5: POSSIBLE RISKS OF BITCOIN

We have just spent some time talking about all of the good benefits that come with Bitcoin. Many people all around the world have joined this network because it provides them with a lot of benefits. They can make purchases and send money all throughout the world, they can remain anonymous on the network, and they can save money on transaction fees.

But despite all of the good things that are available with Bitcoin, it is important to understand that there are a few risks that come with this kind of currency, no matter who you are when you are using it. Some people get into the market because they heard that Bitcoin was a good idea, but you do need to be careful and do some of your own research. Some of the risks that come with Bitcoin include:

Volatile market

The market of Bitcoin is still very volatile. You can look at some of the trends that are going on in the market, and it is not too hard to tell what is going on. Yes, the momentum has been going up, but there are still some large swings of going down as well. No one really knows for sure how this market is going to behave in the future, and that can be a scary thing for a lot of people.

Until the Bitcoin network learns how to even out a little bit better, it is going to be a big risk to join it. You never know how much your money is going to be worth from day to day, and this is not a good thing whether you are a company that accepts Bitcoin, a shopper on the network, or even someone who is interested in investing in this currency.

If you are investing, make sure that you take the proper time to do your research before joining. And you need to watch out for some of those ups and downs in the market. If you just jump in because someone says it is a good idea, you could easily panic and lose out on everything because you see a downward turn. These are going to happen, so prepare yourself for them, have a plan of attack, and know when the market has gone down enough that you should exit it.

Some sellers are not legitimate

One of the big reasons that a lot of people choose to go with the Bitcoin network is because they can shop with ease on this network. They can find some of their favorite retailers that they have loved in the past, or they go on the exchange (kind of like what Craigslist is like) and find sellers for other products that they would like.

For the most part, the people that you work with on these sites will be just fine, and you will be able to transfer the payment over to them and get the product you are looking for. On the other hand, there are also sellers out there who are just trying to take your money and will not provide you with any of the products that you are looking for.

You have to be a smart shopper before you choose to use this kind of network. There aren't really any protections on your money in this network; you have to be careful about it. Make sure to look at the reputation of the seller, talk to them a bit, and get a feel for whether or not they are someone that you are willing to work with.

The market could crash

The Bitcoin network is still pretty new. It has only been around since 2009, which means there hasn't been much of a history to see how it will perform over the long term. And since it is one of the first digital currencies, it is hard to compare it with some of the other online currencies either.

Without this background to help figure out how well the market will do in different economies and over the long-term, it is hard to predict how it is going to work in the future. Sure, right now it is pretty popular and seems to be growing, but there have already been some downward turns that could be alarming.

The future of Bitcoin and the other digital currencies is still uncertain so figuring out how this is going to change in the future, and whether or not the network is going to be around and popular in the next few years and be scary for some people to use. It could be something that sticks around for the long term, or it could be something that will disappear in the near future. Without a history of past performance to go off of, it will be really hard to figure it all out.

No government funding behind it

While some people enjoy the fact that there isn't really a government agency that is controlling their money, there could be some issues that come with doing this as well. Think about some of the big banks that we work with. on a daily basis. Part of the reason that we have so much trust in these big banks is that we know that there is some government funding behind it. If the bank does something wrong or it goes under because of the economy, the government is going to be right there to give us our money back. We will not lose out because we decided to put our money in with a big bank, and it will always be secure.

On the other hand, this is not something that you can expect when it comes to Bitcoin. There isn't a government agency that is behind the coins, and you have no insurance. If Bitcoin starts to fail, you will have to either get your money out quickly and take a loss, hope that the value of Bitcoin will go up even further, or keep in the market and lose everything. No one is going to bail you out. the worry about not being bailed out from whatever can happen with the Bitcoin network is enough to keep some people from putting their money into the market.

As you can see, there are a few downsides to choosing to go with the Bitcoin network. While it can be a great way for you to make money and even to purchase goods and services without the slow ledgers that come with most traditional banks, there is a level of risk that comes each time that you use the system. You have to worry about the system staying available, how the value of the coins will do in the future, and so much more. These factors should really come into play before you decide to join the Bitcoin network.

CHAPTER 6: DO THE BENEFITS OUTWEIGH THE RISKS

Many people wonder whether the benefits of using Bitcoin really outweigh the risks. Is it really worth your time to work with this kind of currency, a currency that does not have the insurance of a big bank or government agency behind it to make sure that your money is safe and one that may just be a fad and all the money will be gone in a few days?

The choice of whether the benefits outweigh the risks is really going to depend on your own personal needs. Some people like the idea of working with Bitcoin. They are happy that they can shop online without having to worry about whether someone can see their transactions or take their money. They like to have a currency that does not have a lot of government interference inside of it.

There really are a lot of benefits that come with using this kind of technology. It can save you money if you are someone who likes to shop in other countries online or if you need to send money to a family member somewhere else. And the transactions are fast, taking just a few minutes to complete rather than having to wait a few days for the transactions to be done with.

As a regular consumer who has decided to work with Bitcoin, it can be a wonderful tool to use. When it comes to the purchases that you are doing online, you can just act like you are using your credit card or your bank account and not have to worry about anything else that is going on behind the scenes. Thanks to the blockchain technology, you will get all of your transactions done quickly and securely without any issues.

Of course, there are some people who may need to be careful about using Bitcoin. Some investors may want to be a bit wary about using this kind of technology because we really do not know how long it is going to stick around. It may look like a technology that is growing, but it does not really have the track record behind it to prove that it will be here for the long term. This can be challenging for some people who want to jump on board.

With traditional investments, it is easy to look back at a long history of stocks and how companies are doing. You can check out how the economy is doing, how the particular company is doing, and other information to see whether a stock is going to be the right one for you.

This is not something that you can do when you are working with the Bitcoin network. This network was developed in 2009, so it is less than ten years old. In addition, it has only started to gain in popularity over the past few years. This does not leave a lot of options when it comes to how much history you can look back at.

You could choose to join the Bitcoin network, but how successful are you going to be? How long is the market going to keep going up for you to earn money in the process? Since there isn't a long history of Bitcoin, there really isn't anything that is going to show whether this investment is going to remain steady or not. It could keep going up, it could remain steady, or it could take a big nosedive in the near future. As the investor, you have to make sound decisions to ensure that your money stays safe.

Some businesses may also want to be careful about working with Bitcoin. Right now, it is widely popular all throughout the world, which means that you will be able to find a lot of customers who use it. Choosing to go with Bitcoin could help you to make more money because you will reach a larger demographic in the process. On the other hand, you could run into issues. What if the Bitcoin network crashes in the near future? You may have some Bitcoin still in your wallet, that you accepted as a form of payment, that would now be considered worthless because of the coin is worthless. This could be a big blow to any company that decided to trade and accepts Bitcoin as a form of payment.

Right now, the market in Bitcoin is doing well. The price is rising, and there are a lot of ways that you can make money and use the coins. However, it is important to watch the market and see what is happening. The Bitcoin market is still pretty new, and you do not want to jump in without fully understanding what is going on around you. For some people staying with the Bitcoin network will be a great option with lots of benefits, but for others, you need to weigh the risks.

PART 3:

HOW DO YOU GET

BITCOINS?

CHAPTER 7: SETTING UP YOUR WALLET AND PURCHASING BITCOIN

The main way that people choose to get Bitcoin is to open up an account with an exchange service and then to exchange some of their traditional currency to get the Bitcoin that they would like to use. There are a few different types of exchanges that you can work with, and they are all meant to make it as easy as possible to get the Bitcoin that you would like to work with.

Coinbase is one of the biggest Bitcoin exchange sites that you can work with. It is available in many countries throughout the world, and it is set up to make things easier for a beginner. They also work with LiteCoin and Ethereum as well so you have some options.

Many beginners like this option for a few reasons. First, it is easy to set up an account. You just need some basic information, such as your name and email address. It also provides you with a wallet that you can store the Bitcoin in and you can complete your online transactions right from there. It is important to note that your Bitcoin address, when provided through Coinbase, is not going to be as secure as the others because they will just use your first and last name. You can always change to a new wallet later on.

So, let's say that you want to purchase Bitcoin through the Coinbase system to keep things simple. The other exchange sites work in a similar manner so you can follow these instructions for that as well. First, you have to take the time to set up your

Coinbase account. You can visit www.coinbase.com to get started on this. They will ask a few questions such as your name and require you to read through the Terms and Conditions before you continue. You can also choose whether you would like to use this account as a personal account or a business account so you can pick from that as well. Verification can go through your email address or your phone number so make sure to provide ones that you use often.

After you have set up your account, you will be directed to the Dashboard. The main page will show you the current value of Bitcoin as well as some of the other popular digital currencies and a little history about how they have been doing recently. This is good information to check out before you make any purchases.

Now it is time to add in a payment method. You have

to use some of your traditional currency to purchase Bitcoin in the beginning, so you have to add in a payment method to make this happen. There are a few options that you can choose from including your bank account, your PayPal account, and even a credit card.

There are some benefits that come with using each of these methods. Some people like to go after their bank accounts because these allow for higher rates of exchanges than the other methods, but it will take three to five days for the transfers to complete so it kind of depends on how long you would like to wait and how much money you want to transfer over.

On the other hand, PayPal and credit cards can transfer the money over instantly. If you would like to be able to work with Bitcoin right away without all of the waits, then this is the right option for you.

The limit amounts for exchanging are much lower with these options, so you have to remember that you will not be able to work with as much in the beginning.

After you have picked out the payment method that you would like to use, your money is going to be added to your Coinbase wallet. Some people decide to keep the money in that wallet because they feel that it is safe or it is the easiest method for them to use. On the other hand, whether or not the Coinbase wallet is that safe is still debatable. Some people choose to move the money over to another wallet that has some special features or some more security based on their needs.

When you have your coins, and you have chosen the wallet that you would like to use, you can start making your purchases and sending money to other people as you would like. The shopping method is pretty simple, just working like your regular bank account but it will rely on the coins that you keep in your wallet.

CHAPTER 8: MINING FOR BITCOIN

Another way that you can make sure that you earn some Bitcoin is to become a miner. This method is a bit harder to complete because you have to have some technical knowledge. These miners are responsible for making sure that the integrity of the system is upheld, so everyone knows their transactions are safe.

When you join the Bitcoin network, you will receive a block. This block will hold all of the transactions that you complete on the Bitcoin network. Some people who work on a lot of transactions will fill up this block pretty quickly, and those who are only on the network on occasion will take longer.

Once the block is all filled up, it is going to become a part of the permanent record. It will join the other blocks that you have filled up over time to form your own personal blockchain. In addition, it will also join the main blockchain on the Bitcoin network, so it is secure with all of the other transactions as well.

The goal of the miner is to help keep these blocks safe. They are going to be in charge of creating unique hashes that will hide the information that is inside of these blocks. Of course, there are some rules about making these hashes, or else everyone would choose to write them, and everything would be taken too early on in the game.

One of the rules that come with these hashes is that there need to be a certain amount of zeroes at the beginning of the hash. And each hash has to line up with the one that came before it. This makes it difficult, but it helps because it ensures that if someone tries to mess with the system, they are going to change up everything, making it easy for everyone to notice that someone was messing around.

Since it is impossible to know what the hash is going to look like ahead of time, it can take some time to create these hashes. Some miners do have a computer program to help them out, but it will just produce the hashes, and they have to figure out which ones will meet up with the requirements of the Bitcoin network.

This is meant to be a little bit difficult to accomplish because it is meant to help keep the information safe. No one will be able to see your personal information inside of the block so it will help keep the hackers out. The blockchain, as well as the work that the miners do, come together to ensure that the Bitcoin network will stay as safe as possible.

Because the work of the miners is so difficult, they are going to be rewarded for their work. Right now they can earn 25 Bitcoin for each hash that they complete successfully. Since each Bitcoin is currently worth $3500, this is a good reward for getting the work done. This helps to incentive them to do the work and will keep the network as safe as possible.

You have to remember that mining is going to be good for both parties. It does take some work though. The Bitcoin network made it hard for a number of reasons. The first reason is that they wanted to make sure that the information stayed safe. If there weren't some tough protocols in place for the process of mining, it would be really easy for someone to mess around with the blockchain ledger and change up whatever information they wanted. The trust in the blockchain network would disappear, and no one would want to use this system.

In addition, if it were easy to set up a Bitcoin hash, it would not take long until everyone decided to jump on board. Since you can earn 25 Bitcoin for each time, this is done, and with Bitcoin being worth over $3500 each, it is easy to see that a lot of people would decide to jump on this opportunity and try to make some money in the process. With adding in some challenges to creating these hashes, not only does the Bitcoin network make sure that the transactions stay safe and sound, but it also ensures that all of the coins on the network are not mined overnight.

The work of the miner is not always easy. You have to have some computer knowledge to get this done and a lot of patience. But if you are willing to work hard and keep at it, you can earn a great reward of Bitcoins, without having to use your own money, and you get the benefit of knowing that you helped to keep the Bitcoin network safe.

PART 4:

USING BITCOIN

CHAPTER 9: HOW DO YOU USE BITCOIN

One question that you may have is how you can use Bitcoin. It is actually pretty easy to use Bitcoin, and you can use it just like you would with a credit card or other form of payment. The biggest difference is that you will not be able to print off the money and use it at a physical store.

You can imagine this like making transactions out of your own bank account. You can transfer the money anywhere that you would like, or anywhere that the money is accepted, to make your purchases, send money to other people, and more.

Use at your favorite stores

The first way that you can use Bitcoin is at some of your favorite stores. There are a lot of stores that are already accepting Bitcoin. They recognize that there is a big demand for these coins and if they choose to accept these Bitcoins, it will be easier for them to reach a larger target audience.

Before you go shopping on the Bitcoin network, first check out which of your favorite stores already accept Bitcoin. You may be surprised at how many stores accept this as a form of payment, just like with PayPal and credit cards.

If your favorite shop already accepts Bitcoin, the work is going to be pretty easy to work with. You simply need to do your shopping and then click on the link to pay with Bitcoin. Once you do this, the seller will send you a link to their Bitcoin wallet. You just transfer the money right over, and you will be all set to go. The seller is going to send over the product that you ordered as soon as they receive their coins, which will only take a few minutes.

Purchase gift cards

Now, not all of the stores that you want to shop at are going to accept Bitcoin. Is growing in popularity, but not every store has decided to accept this as a form of payment. It is still possible to shop with your coins at these stores; you just get to be more creative about how you do it.

Working with gift cards is a fantastic way to make this happen. Let's look at an example of how this would work. Amazon.com is a big online retailer, but they do not work with Bitcoin at all. Instead of avoiding this website altogether, you can go online and purchase some Bitcoins.

There are a few websites online that accept Bitcoin

and will give you an online gift card to some of your favorite stores. You could use your Bitcoin to purchase an Amazon.com gift card and then take it to the website to make a purchase later on. It is not the most direct way to make a purchase, but it still allows you a chance to make purchases with your Bitcoin.

Making purchases with Bitcoin is pretty easy to work with. You can use it like you do any other type of payment that you would do online. This makes it easy for you to do all of your purchases on the Bitcoin network.

Sending money

Some people decide to use Bitcoin to send money to people throughout the world. This can be a really challenging and expensive process when you use a traditional banking method. You have to always worry about the exchange rate, and then the third parties that you work with are going to decide to charge you a fee on top of everything. This makes the whole exchange more expensive, and no one wants to deal with that when they are trying to send friends and family members some money.

This is not an issue when you decide to work with Bitcoin. You do not need to worry about the exchange rate at all because you can just send over the coins and the other person will have them available. You can do all of this instantly, so there isn't an issue with exchange rates at all and since you are relying on the blockchain platform, you get the added benefit of not having to worry about adding to a third party. As long as you have a Bitcoin address, a wallet, and some money already available, you can get all of this done in just a few minutes whenever you would like.

Make money

Another method that you can try out is to make your own money with Bitcoin. If you already have your own business, you can do this without having to spend any money at all. You can just join the Bitcoin network and get the address that you would like, set up a wallet, and then set it up on your website so that your customers can choose to pay in Bitcoin as they choose.

Whenever a customer wants to pay in Bitcoin, you would just need to send them information about your Bitcoin address, and they can send the money right over. You can then use these coins to make other purchases or exchange them out for the traditional currency that you like to use, depending on your needs.

As you can see, there are a lot of different options for getting the Bitcoin that you would like to use. Take some time to pick the ones that you would like to read to help you get started.

CHAPTER 10: IS BITCOIN SECURE?

One question that a lot of people have when they are first getting started with the Bitcoin is whether this form of currency is actually going to keep their information secure or not. This is supposed to be one of the benefits of working with this kind of technology, but how secure is your information in real life?

Most people have spent some time doing shopping online. They are used to being able to make purchases and send money to any seller that they want online. They would use their bank information or their credit card numbers to get this work done. It is an efficient system, but it is not always one that is the most secure.

How often do you turn on the news or look online and see that there was another hacking attack? Usually, this is going to be with a big company or a big bank that is supposed to keep personal and payment information safe from hackers. Now that the hacker can get onto the network, they can gain access to names, phone numbers, addresses, and credit card information for all of the people who trusted that company.

With these hacks occurring all of the time, it is no

wonder that people have a hard time trusting online shopping. There are very few, if any, people who have been able to shop online without their information being compromised at all.

There are a lot of different reasons that people would choose to want to keep their information hidden. We already spent some time talking about one of the reasons, keeping their personal and payment information hidden while they are online. But there are a number of other reasons that people like to make sure that their information is hidden online as well including:

- Do transactions without others finding out
- Keeping their credit cards safe from fraud
- Keeping other people out of their transactions, like the government.
- More freedom when they are shopping online.

- Not having to worry about the big data breaches that occur almost every day now.

Most companies are not able to provide this kind of safety and security to their customers. No matter how much they promise that they are using the newest safety features, they often end up falling short.

But Bitcoin has made some claims about helping people to keep their information safe. The real question is though, is this network really able to make sure that your personal and payment information will stay away from people who should not see it?

There are a few ways that you will be able to do this. The first comes in the form of the blockchain. This technology is set up to keep your information safe.

When it enters into the ledger on the blockchain network, you do not have to worry about people being able to see the information. You can always check the information and make sure that it is right, but if someone else came in, they would see your unique Bitcoin address (which hopefully does not have your personal first and last name on it) and then a unique hash that the miners were responsible for creating.

Now, it is important that you are still careful with the things that you do on this Bitcoin network. There are hackers out there who would love to get ahold of your personal information and start to take away your Bitcoins if they had a chance. This means that you need to take some extra precautions when you are doing purchases and other transactions.

If a hacker was really interested in it, they would be

able to take a look at the blockchain and see some of the transactions that are going on. If you were doing a lot of transactions at the same time at the same place, they might be able to use that information to figure out who you are.

This would take them a little bit of time to complete, but it is something that they would be able to do if they chose. Just like with some of the other shopping methods that you may have used in the past, you have to be someone who can handle your transactions online, choose reputable sellers that will not give away your information, and make sure that you are discrete as possible.

There are a few things that you can do I needed to help make sure that your transactions are as safe as possible. For someone who will use their Bitcoin quite a bit, it is recommended that you change out your address after each transaction. This is going to guarantee that no one is going to be able to figure out who you are when you do transactions on this network.

Now, most people will not want to spend the time to change out their Bitcoin address each time that they want to do a new transaction, especially if they like to do a lot of activity on this network. It is fine if you do not switch it out each time, but try to set up some schedule where you are not using the same code too many times in a row. The more times that you use the same address, and with the higher frequency, the easier it will be for a hacker to get on and figure out who you are.

PART 5:

MAKING MONEY

FROM BITCOIN

CHAPTER 11: BEST WAYS TO MAKE MONEY WITH BITCOIN

There are a lot of different reasons to join the Bitcoin network. Some people will choose to do this to send money to other countries. Some like that it is easy to use and that they can finish up transactions in just a few minutes rather than having to wait a few days for it to go through. Still, others are fans of being able to stay hidden with their transactions online, keeping them safe from hackers and other people online.

It is also possible to join this network to make money. Some people have seen all of the value that comes with Bitcoin, and they have chosen to join the network to make some money on this system. And there are a few different options that you can try out to help with the idea of investing your Bitcoin. Some of the methods that you can try out include:

Invest in the Bitcoin network

The Bitcoin company is actually available on a few different trading sites, and this can be a great way for you to earn some money. If you have some experience with the stock market, it is fine for you to go onto NASDAQ and trade in this company. Just like with some other stocks, you will be able to earn a quarterly dividend when the stocks are doing well. And since Bitcoin is so valuable and growing in popularity right now, so you can earn some good returns on this investment.

Day trading

One option that some people like to work with is day

trading. Day trading allows you to make a lot of small sales all throughout the day. You will not make a lot of profit all at once, but if you do this throughout the day, you will end up making some good money.

With this option, you will make a purchase of the Bitcoin when the price is low during the day, and then you sell it later in the day when the price goes up. The trick here is to remember to sell before you go to sleep at night. The Bitcoin network is running all throughout the world, so it really does not have a closing day like other stocks. That means a lot can happen if you go to bed without selling your coins.

Invest in the blockchain technology

Another place where you can invest in the Bitcoin network is with the blockchain technology.

Blockchain is one of the underlying technologies that are behind Bitcoin, helping to keep things in order and to provide a ledger for all of the transactions that occur on the network. Without it, Bitcoin would have some trouble running properly. But Bitcoin is not the only application that blockchain will work with. Blockchain can have a lot of other applications, which makes it perfect to invest in.

Many people are investing in new blockchain platforms to use with digital voting, smart contracts, insurance, and the finance industry. There are many options, and the companies who are developing this kind of technology need funding to help them out. This could be the perfect option for you when it comes to investing.

Buy and hold

Buy and hold is a good option to use as a beginner. It is pretty simple to work with, but you need to have the patience to stick around and let it work. The daily fluctuations in the value of Bitcoin can make this one hard for some people. The price may go down for a little bit at times, but it has a steady upward trend. If you jump out of the market too quickly, you could end up losing money rather than making any.

This method is pretty simple to work with. You will start by opening up your own Bitcoin account and finding an exchange rate that you want to work with. Coinbase is a good one to work with, but you can choose another type of exchange if you would like. Once your account is set up, just exchange your traditional currency for the Bitcoin.

These Bitcoins need to be left in your wallet for some time. You should come up with a backup of your coins just in case something does happen. The coins will just need to sit inside of the wallet for some time until you reach your goal for income. Once this happens, you will exchange your Bitcoins back out for regular coins, and you can keep the profit.

Sell your own products

We have touched on this one a little bit inside of this guidebook, but another option that you may want to discuss is to sell your own products. If you already have a business online that you are selling from, why not accept Bitcoin as a form of payment. This is not going to cost you any more money to accomplish, but it will open up your target market to more people and can help you get secure payments in just a few minutes.

To start adding Bitcoin as a form of accepted payment, you first need to set up your own wallet and make sure that it is set up as a business account. You can then add a button onto your storefront that lets others know that you will accept their Bitcoin for the products that you are selling.

When a seller is interested in purchasing something using their Bitcoins, they will simply need to press the button that you added. You can send them your Bitcoin address, they can transfer the payment over to you, and then the process is done. The money will be in your own wallet quickly so that you can send the product out to your customer. It is as easy as that!

As you can see, there are quite a few different ways

that you can make a profit when you join the Bitcoin network. Try out a few of these options and see which one works the best for you.

PART 6:

BLOCKCHAIN

BASICS

Chapter 12: Investments with Block Chain

The business models of several different companies in a wide range of sectors have been transformed by block chain. Looking at block chain, you are going to see that it appears to be a digital spreadsheet that is being worked on by members inside of an organization. The "digital spreadsheet" is going to be on a decentralized network.

Due to the way that block chain is written, it has some unique factors that are not going to be able to be understood, even by the investors that think that they can make a profit on that technology. Block chain is not like traditional trading because it has several different levels that are used.

Block chain offers at least five different ways that you can make an investment that will benefit you later on.

1. Stockpile coins

Many investors are stockpiling gold so that they can wait to sell it whenever the price goes up sometime in the future. However, there are other investors that are stockpiling bitcoins. Stockpiling gold and stockpiling bitcoins are going to each have their advantages as well as their disadvantages but what it comes down to is the supply and demand. Whenever the supply is limited, the demand is going to go up, therefore, the value is going to increase which is going to be the opportune time to sell what it is that they are stockpiling.

2. Penny stocks

Penny stocks are a cryptocurrency like bitcoins just like Ether is a cryptocurrency, but they all work on a different system due to the fact that they are competing with bitcoin.

3. Crowdfunding with altcoin

Crowdfunding is a method that you can use whenever you are trying to raise capital for an investment. The coins are not going to need to be used when you are dealing with crowdfunding.

Instead, people are going to give you coins before you start mining which is typically done before a system is opened to the public.

4. Angel funding and start up ventures

Block chain makes it possible for a great number of entrepreneurs and investors to come together and find each other to get funding.

5. Pure block chain technology

The technology behind block chain is on the rise, and the companies that are taking advantage of it are getting their name out there so that they can be better known whenever you find the block chain technology everywhere. A company by the name of Global Arena Holdings uses the block chain technology as leverage in getting their votes verified.

Chapter 13: Implementing Block Chain

Knowing how you want to use block chain is vital before you get too deep into it. Block chain offers two ways to use their system, but ensure that you are choosing the one that is best for you. Typically people use block chain with an individual account.

With an individual account, you need to set up your wallet. Your wallet is going to be where you keep all of your bitcoins and will run off of most mobile devices and computers. Digital wallets are more secure than real wallets because they are not going to be stolen and they are most likely not going to be hacked.

When you use a software wallet, you are not going to be required to have a third party service for the wallet to be downloaded. Once it has been placed on your computer, you are going to have all of your transactions at your fingertips.

Next, you need to acquire bitcoins. You have the option to trade bitcoins for goods or services that you may be able to offer to those in the bitcoin system; however, it is hard to find someone who is willing to trade bitcoins because they do not want to give up their coins. You can also buy bitcoins in the marketplace where you can spend real world money and purchase as many coins as you want.

Lastly, you have the option to mine coins. Programs can be placed on your computer that will use a CPU that is customized to assist you in making a quick profit without you having to do many of anything.

You should make sure that your wallet is secured! Encrypt your wallet so that you are not leaving it open to hackers who want to steal your coins. If your coins are stolen, or bitcoin does not offer you an option where they will replace them because they are your responsibility.

Bitcoins can be spent just like regular money can be.

However, you need to find a merchant who will accept bitcoins as payment.

Chapter 14: Smart Contracts

Smart contracts are probably going to be the aspect of block chain that will most likely be championed in the future. A smart contract is just a type of computer code that is activated once the block chain as a whole register that a predetermined incident has occurred. The smart contract is then given its own block and distributed as part of the chain.

While it may seem complicated, you can think of them in much the same way certain functions in a checking account work. In most checking accounts, automated deductions can be set up either by the user or by a third party with the user's permission. A smart contract works in broadly the same way but from a decentralized—not centralized--position. Put another way; a smart contract is the computer code equivalent of the legalese in a contract that stipulates how and when all the little details are carried out.

Additionally, as long as the smart contract is generated on a public block chain, then, unlike in the banking example, there is no third party (such as the bank) who is able to step in and actively prevent the transaction from occurring. The transaction is equally secure if it is performed by a bank or by a block chain. This is due to the extreme type of security that is built into the block chain model, the fact that the data is decentralized, and the extreme cost required to hijack a block chain.

What's more, unlike with traditional contracts, smart contracts that are executed via block chain are completely public and viewable by anyone with a copy of the chain. This means that the smart contract is never open for debate or discussion; it is purely an expression of the facts as they are truly stated. This can be seen as a miracle or a curse, of course, depending on the nature of the information being made public.

A smart contract is where a computer protocol can facilitate, verify, and even enforce the negotiation and performance of a contract in which the contractual clause becomes unnecessary.

The smart contract can also have a user interface that will emulate the logic of a contractual clause(s). The proponents of a smart contract claim that many different kinds of the contractual clauses may thus be made partial or even fully self-executing, self-enforcing, or possibly even both.

Smart contracts are going to aim to provide the security that is superior to any traditional law contract. This will, therefore, reduce the transaction costs that are associated with the process of drawing up a contract.

Common usage cases

With the rising market penetration of various financial technologies, smart contracts are becoming more and more prevalent. A big reason for that is because they are simplifying many common contract usage cases. For example, they are already making it easier for users to update various contract terms in real time, despite it taking days for physical copies to move back and forth to perform the same function. This not only improves the speed with which such processes can be performed but also greatly increases the odds of their accuracy remaining at acceptable levels throughout.

Smart contracts also activate automatically once certain real world conditions have been met, which means they require fewer resources to be utilized to the fullest. While this won't mean much to most users who use them infrequently, for business to business transactions, the savings will likely be substantial. The guaranteed and secure nature of a smart contract also means that it can be executed upon without the need for a third party to guarantee the transaction via escrow, reducing the closing costs of the contract on all sides.

Financial institutions will also find smart contracts useful in numerous ways. In regard to trade clearing or settlement scenarios, the final results relating to settlements, transfers, and trades is tallied automatically. Smart contracts can also be used when it comes to coupon payments, specifically to return principal on expired bonds. They also work with insurance claims as a means of minimizing errors and streamlining the flow of work between departments. Finally, they are also known to improve the regulation of Internet of Things services.

In the health care sector, smart contracts are known to offer up numerous advantages. For instance, they improve the accuracy with which medical records are updated as patients are transferred between departments. They can also be used to monitor the health of the population as a whole via public blockchains that update automatically and pay participants for using their information. Smart contracts are also already in use in many Internet of Things devices where they are used to determine the success of fitness goals and release rewards accordingly.

In the music industry, smart contracts are already being put to work tracking royalties for song usage and distributing payments accordingly. It is also being put to work on a smaller scale to enhance person to person interactions and is predicted to lead to things like trading energy credits and increased peer lending opportunities. This same technology is currently being adapted for use with the Tesla electric car, whereby users can charge at any charging station and be billed for the transaction automatically.

It is also changing the way large products are shipped and tracked by sending out automated documentation as various production pieces make their way through processing, and on to shipping. This can even be cued to the input of certain signatures, meaning the process is seamless for signing the contract to receiving the goods. Later on down the line, if there are questions about the quality of the shipment, then the entire route the product took from creation to delivery can be tracked. This is due to the fact that it is on the same block chain that enables the creation of the contract in the first place.

For credit enforcement, the smart contracts are becoming an extension of property law. The credit agreements are going to disable the product that you have purchased if you fail to make the payments that you agreed to make. For example, if you buy a new car on credit and fail to make your payment. Then the doors to your car are going to lock and then drive itself back to the showroom.

However, most electrical products come with what is known as a kill switch that can be disabled should a condition not be met between the two parties. This would happen if the payments were being made through a public channel such as cryptocurrency.

Chapter 15: Block Chain Pros and Cons

Block chain is not immune to have its pros and cons just like everything else that you can get involved in. While block chain is versatile, there are still those who are hesitant to switch over to the new technology when they can just stick to the methods they know work.

Block chain will protect your identity as well as work with you to make sure that your money is not stolen. Your personal information does not have to be entered into the block chain system in order for any transactions to be completed. It is going to be much like when you buy something with cash. You do not even have to enter a real email address. The block chain system gives you an email address, so that will change each time that you make a transaction on the system.

If there is any cost to send or receive a payment on

the block chain system, it is not going to be a large fee. Any payments that go international will not force you to pay things such as transaction or exchange fees that a traditional financial institute would force you to do. Therefore, this will help keep all of your fees down when you find yourself traveling abroad.

One of the biggest cons that you are going to find with block chain is that you do not have the ability to reverse a transaction once you have made it. So, you need to be cautious when you are sending out coins because once it has been spent, there is a possibility that you are not going to get a refund from that person. Basically, keep a good handle on where you send your coins and have extra security on your system so that your coins cannot be stolen by a hacker.

Keeping your bitcoins means that you are going to have to deal with volatility. The value of bitcoins fluctuates with time and the longer you hold onto them, the less value they are going to hold when you are ready to spend them. So, you are going to be gambling with your coins and their value the longer that you hold onto them.

There are several companies such as Etsy and TigerDirect that are going to accept bitcoins as a form of payment rather than taking cash. However, big companies like Walmart and Target have not gotten on board yet, and there is no telling when they are going to get on board with bitcoin considering how well they are doing as it is. But, it is very likely that they are going to look into accepting bitcoins as the value of bitcoins goes up making it to where more and more people are using it.

Rather than being like a credit card, bitcoins are like cash. There are no extensions in the warranty that you have to deal with, but then again you are not going to have the rewards that you can get when it comes to using a credit card. Some places do not allow you to use a credit card for whatever policy reason that they have so then you are always going to worry about that as well. Then there are the fees and the added headache of if you do not pay it, it is going to affect your credit score.

Cash, on the other hand, is taken everywhere, there are no fees, in fact, there are many times that you end up getting a discount because you used cash. With bitcoin, you are going to be able to use it without the headache of late fees or other things that you are going to have to worry about with a credit card.

The biggest similarity that bitcoins has with credit cards is the fact that it is not going to be accepted everywhere.

On the business side of it, using bitcoin is going to save you money. If you are going to use services such as Coinbase, then the first million dollars that you make by accepting bitcoins is going to be free for you. It is from here that you are going to begin to pay at least one percent on all of the transactions that you do. However, this is still going to be considerably less than what you are paying in order to accept credit cards.

Exchanges that are doing with bitcoins can be converted easily without the need to worry about risking a lot of volatility. Not to mention, bitcoin eases any worries that you are going to have of chargebacks or even hackers getting into your system and stealing your customer's credit card numbers. The merchants that use bitcoin are normally going to work off of a tablet or even a smartphone when they are accepting a payment. This is an added benefit because you will not need a big fancy system that can only stay in one place. Therefore, you are going to be able to take your business with you anywhere and accept payments. Which is a major plus for your business!

CONCLUSION

There are a lot of people who have decided that Bitcoin is the right currency for them to try out. They are excited to get into something new, something that may not have been tried in the past, and focus their energy on a new type of product and a new way of spending money. It may not be the traditional method that you are used to, but it is certainly an effective and secure method to work with.

This book took some time to talk about Bitcoin and all of the different ways that you can use it. We started out with a quick introduction to how you can get started with Bitcoin, such as what this currency is all about and some of the technology that helps it to run.

We then moved on to some other aspects of this digital currency including some of the positives of using this currency, the negatives of going with it, how to sign up for your own Bitcoin account, how to start spending your money with Bitcoin, and even some of the best ways to invest and make money with this network.

Part of the reason that the Bitcoin network is gaining so much in popularity is that there really is something for everyone to enjoy. Whether you are looking to join this network as a way to make money, to invest, to spend your money securely, or some other method, you will be able to find that when you decide to work with Bitcoin.

We've come to the end of our discussion on Bitcoin, do decide what's right for you moving forward and I wish you the best of luck in all your endeavors.

Till next time,

Jerry Ryder

CPSIA information can be obtained
at www.ICGtesting.com
Printed in the USA
LVHW050230151220
674148LV00020B/4151